"This is a lovely, heart-centered, uplifting offering that can move you to look at your life through new eyes. Bev Mullen has cleverly taken a familiar symbol and turned into a guide for spiritual illumination. Hearty appetite to those who wish to walk the path with heart."

Alan Cohen, author of *A Daily Dose of Sanity*

The Nature of a Complete Thought

As Easy as Pie

Beverley Mullen

BALBOA
PRESS

Balboa Press books may be ordered through booksellers or by contacting:

Balboa Press
A Division of Hay House
1663 Liberty Drive
Bloomington, IN 47403
www.balboapresspress.com
1-(877) 407-4847

Because of the dynamic nature of the Internet, any Web addresses or links contained in this book may have changed since publication and may no longer be valid. The views expressed in this work are solely those of the author and do not necessarily reflect the views of the publisher, and the publisher hereby disclaims any responsibility for them.

ISBN: 978-1-4525-0042-3 (sc)
ISBN: 978-1-4525-0043-0 (e)

Library of Congress Control Number: 2010913968

The author of this book does not dispense medical advice or prescribe the use of any technique as a form of treatment for physical, emotional, or medical problems without the advice of a physician, either directly or indirectly. The intent of the author is only to offer information of a general nature to help you in your quest for emotional and spiritual well-being. In the event you use any of the information in this book for yourself, which is your constitutional right, the author and the publisher assume no responsibility for your actions.

Printed in the United States of America

Balboa Press rev. date: 6/19/2013

Preface

I wrote this book to remind myself
To stop basing my life on everything I hate
And to start living my life through everything I love.

I gave myself:
Pie to keep life delicious, playful, creative, and diverse
Poems to contemplate
Nature to inspire trust in myself
and
Actions that center me back into the love of being me.

And now I give this all to you
Just in case you would like to fill your life with love, too.

Contents

Introduction

There really is nothing better than warm pie, made with love, fresh from the oven. It is a creation you can enjoy over and over. It is good any time of day and can be enjoyed alone or with family and friends; even strangers seem closer to us when sharing pie. It seems like you barely start one pie, and you are already thinking about the next.

Through the metaphor of pie, I hope to escort you on a journey about yourself and where your "today" is leading you. Every person's journey is unique, but each one is perfect and always right on track. We have just forgotten how lovely and enjoyable the experience of life is.

To make a pie, you just work through a few basic steps. First, there is the creative part—choosing the delicious ingredients for the filling and crust. Next, you enjoy the fun of putting it all together and baking it. Lastly, you taste the pie and experience how all this effort has made you feel. The nature of a complete thought works the same way. You decide on an idea, create it, and—through the experience of producing it—you draw a conclusion as to whether or not you enjoyed it, which completes that thought. One completed thought moves on to the next thought, and then to the next. Each completed thought helps build our self-awareness and opens our lives to new inspiration, which ultimately leads us to loving ourselves and the lives we are living.

Clouds

I float beneath you
looking up into your vast world.
You have your own air flow
one I will never feel
but with graceful movements
I see the journey of your tides
fast and wispy
slow and fluffy
light and dark
as you cast upon each other
blending, once separate now joined
no struggle, just a constant
flow and motion, free to transform
constantly and forever.

Ingredients

So, let's get started. Just as in making a pie, we need to get out the ingredients. We need to find where we are in life and where we could be heading. It is very important to note that if you aren't honest with yourself about your ingredients, the flavor of your life will not be to your liking. There is no point in making strawberry pie when you really love raspberry. Your personal "ingredients" might look like the last few books or magazines you've read. For some people, listing their ingredients is an easy task; they just look at their bedside table, and, *hello*, there's a stack of books. Now, don't roll your eyes. If you are not a book lover, just list your favorite movies or TV shows; or, if your life is more energetic than that, choose a sport you play or watch.

Really, the point is just to think about the things you love. You can pick any combination of activities that you spend your time on. Now is the time to be honest with yourself about what you really enjoy. For some this will be a little harder, because each day is so full of activity that they have never really contemplated what actions or activities they do repeatedly for enjoyment. Let's face it: Even if every day is jam-packed with life, there are still little things you do to make yourself feel comforted or happy or to provide an escape. It might be playing with the kids; or maybe it really is baking pie.

Teacher

The "ingredients" I have surrounded myself with are my favorite books by Eckhart Tolle, Byron Katie, Antoine De Saint-Exupery, and Esther and Jerry Hicks. Do you notice a theme? They are all spiritual or self-improvement books. Next, I'm adding my favorite radio programs: Hay House radio and Oprah on XM radio. And then there's my favorite movie, *The Matrix*. (Would you have guessed that one?) Last July, I started a new activity—meditation. If I did not know myself better, I would say I have a one-track mind.

I must say that Daniel, who is the love of my life, makes it pretty easy to see where his thoughts are focused. The magazines he goes for are: *Sport Diver, National Geographic, Scuba Diver,* and *Sailing*. His favorite movies are *Master and Commander* and *The Big Blue*. You can guess the activities he loves: scuba diving, sailing, and swimming.

But what about you? What ingredients have you noticed in your life? What is always calling for your attention? Gardening, needlepoint, golf, four-wheeling, hunting, collecting miniatures, playing games, daydreaming about great vacations—they all count. Do you see any similarities in your choices?

Sometimes, we hide our ingredients from ourselves. We think we are not worthy; or we think others will mock us or even take our ingredients away from us. We think they can be stolen or ruined by another. Thankfully, even if we have hidden them, they are still somewhere inside of us. So, remember to look internally, too.

May I be so bold as to share one of my dreams with you? I think it expands on this point and helps explain it better.

Nature

There was a snapping sound, and I turned to see you bent over a broken twig in the still water. You were a stunning tree with delicate spring blossoms, your flowers a deep magenta that faded out to the palest pink.

In your reflection, you were reminded of your beauty, and anger rose within you. Your pain-filled words spilled out. Others admired only your radiance; your external beauty was all that they saw or cared about, nothing more. No one appreciated all your other gifts—like the shelter you provided for birds, squirrels, and too many bugs to name. Nor could they see or understand the strength, depth, and complexity of your roots. The fierceness of your speech turned your leaves dry and brittle. Your rage swirled around you, pulling you apart. You seemed to shatter in that instant: a pile of dried leaves, each leaf a moment in your life, all your stories in a jumbled mess. Through your tears you cursed your own beauty. The emptiness that now filled you was threatening to take your last breath.

Your sorrow washed over me, and I frantically tried to piece you back together; but each leaf was a personal story, and, as hard as I tried, I could make no sense of it. There was no flow. The sharp edges pricked my fingers as if mocking me. Your trunk had become a translucent white with merely a hint of color. Trying to hang on, your eyes searched mine, asking, pleading, *Why could they only see my beauty?*

I drew a long, slow breath; and then, I let my hands follow my heart's guidance and place your leaves as they willed. I did not want to lose you, so I distracted you from your rage by telling you my own story, as that is the only story we each may know. In trying to comfort you, I explained that I thought my troubles came from outside of me. I told how some of my branches had been snapped off, and that, whenever a branch broke, I would inevitably notice someone close to me and blame it on them. It seemed to make sense that this person must have done it. I even asked around: Wasn't it true that the people closest to you hurt you the most? Everyone agreed.

Then, one day, someone very close to me cracked off one of my oldest limbs, and I, like you, was instantly enraged. I, too, yelled, *Look what you have done to me! You are so thoughtless, so unkind. If you loved me, you would not be able to do this to me; you have no respect; you don't really see me or care for me.* The words just kept flying out of me. Each was mean, and I wanted to hurt him as much as I thought he had hurt me. He became confused, ashamed, and remorseful; but he did not know how to fix what he had done. So he ran away.

Alone, I now had time to think, something I had not been doing. I always just reacted to everything. I looked at the broken branch. I knew I had many strong branches. I would be fine without this one. As I slowly turned the broken bough in my hands, my mind opened up, and I saw the branch differently, as if for the first time. I realized the limb was already damaged from the inside. There was something more at work here. I had stopped the flow of sap. I might have done it last year or ten years ago, but the fact was that I had made this happen. I had made this weakness a part of me. The branch had broken, because someone close to me had put pressure on it. It was unavoidable. Dead branches always snap under pressure.

So, it was not someone else's fault! I dug deep into my soul to see what reason I would have to weaken myself in this way. I was so overjoyed to discover that the answer was within myself. For my whole life, I had been growing boughs in every direction. Some were big and strong; some were small and flexible; and some I had abandoned, neglected, and withdrawn my attention from. They had become brittle and finally died. I had just never noticed.

I could see now that each branch was an idea, a thought, a dream, or my imagination. I could also see that some ideas were my own, and other thoughts came from people around me. The thoughts I loved most were my strongest, healthiest boughs— with lots of shoots—and I had found additional, similar idea's to sustain them. Some branches were so magnificent, you could swing from them. I could see that other ideas were only of mild interest to me; they had grown, but never really flourished, because I had outgrown or replaced them with something new. Some branches, I had neglected—these were the ideas I had stopped feeding and nurturing, cutting off the sap to them. I had sent the energy somewhere else but was still reluctant to part with the old branch. Within my maze of leaves, flowers, and limbs were my dormant and dead ideas. And, although they meant nothing to me, I was always angered when someone close to me snapped them off. I guess I was being forced to look one last time at something I had forgotten.

So, as life had destined, the very next time someone close to me cracked off one of my branches, I was eager to examine it. This branch was a very old thought; it said that I was not loveable, because I was not perfect. Of course, the snapping of this branch at first confirmed its point. I had always thought perfection was never weak. I smiled to myself, because an old idea had now been removed completely. My smile broadened when I realized that beside this branch had grown a new, thicker, stronger idea that perfection was in everything—even sad and terrible things, like someone close to you breaking your boughs, or people seeing you as one-dimensional, unable to look past your beauty.

My hands came to rest. Even as I shared my thoughts with you, I had been working to piece together your leaves. I looked down at you and realized that you were no longer the flowering tree; instead, you were a sturdy trunk with roots firmly planted in the ground. You stood tall and straight, ready to make a new start on this beautiful spring morning. Next to you, the pond reflected the magenta sunrise, with edges fading out to the palest pink.

This dream may help you understand that some of the ingredients you see around you do not really hold your attention as they once did. Like the dead branches of the tree, we tend to keep old ideas and the items that represent them—just in case, or just to please others. Sometimes, we go looking to make apple-cinnamon-brown sugar pie with ice cream, because everyone loves it. But, one bite into it, our taste buds remind us that we personally prefer mixed-berry pie.

Acknowledge the individual ideas that are working for you. Acknowledge that you are starting to remember what it is you love. Enjoy some mixed-berry pie while you open yourself up to seeing how your true preferences, unbeknownst to you, have worked themselves into your everyday self.

Judgment

When you remembered your love of mixed-berry pie, did you make a quick judgment about all the other flavors? Did you think to yourself, I love mixed-berry pie, it's the best in the world, and no other pie need ever be made again? You may have a list of one hundred reasons why this is so, and another list, just as long, of people that agree with you. You have made up your mind. You will listen to no one. Then, you live for the next thirty years eating only mixed-berry pie. There is no other possibility for you. You have closed off every opportunity for anything different.

But maybe, one day, your granddaughter is eating coconut cream pie. She looks over at you, gives you that look, and, in her own sweet voice, says, "Try some for me. Oh, please.

I hope you are laughing, because kids really do have a way of opening our hearts to something new. Anyway, just like magic, all the pies in the world are open to you again. You no longer have to limit your taste to just one kind. In fact, if you don't judge them at all, then you can have a new preference everyday, and so can the people around you.

I just want to remind you how judgment works. Yes, I know you use it everyday, and we all think it is very helpful; but, really, it can be quite tricky. We confuse personal taste with judgment. Personal taste is knowing what we enjoy, which, of course, can change over time. Judgment is something we use to push against ideas or other people. We judge them on whether they agree or disagree with our personal taste, and, if there is not complete agreement, we start to push.

When we state our opinion to another person regarding anything, all we are doing is confirming our own personal taste, good or bad. As soon as we do that, we stop seeing anything else—like eating only one pie flavor. We focus on our statement, stopping the flow of possibilities. We then internalize the information to see if we can come up with more supporting ideas, more proof that we are correct in our views. The judgment comes when we want others to believe exactly as we do. We try as hard as we can to push our ideas onto them. This puts a stop to the natural flow of our well-being. It also stops us from seeing the other person's point of view. We now see only our own truth—and a person that does not support it. This will be repeated every time we see this person. Every conversation will be another opportunity to prove our point, to try and change that persons mind. Both parties are trapped without possibilities. But, if we don't judge and defend our choices, we are free to change them whenever we like. We are free to have a new conversation with fresh ideas.

There is no greater gift we can give ourselves and others than to try new things, to enjoy sampling the multitude of possibilities around us. Oh, to love the experience of life!

Hoarding

We tend to hoard ideas the same way we do objects. (You should see my pie plate collection.) Take the idea of choosing only one pie, whose flavor will suit us for our whole life. We do the same with love; but, when we hang onto the idea of love, it comes out in tears, because we feel cut-off, removed, or left out.

When we let the love flow through us, feel all its blessings, and find gratitude in difficult moments, then love feels like joy, and one thought builds to the next. The feeling is gratifying and whole; we feel close to everyone—no separation, always connected.

I had been hoarding the idea that I could not be a writer, because I'm dyslexic. Over the years, I lost count of how many tears I've shed over this notion. I have been writing poetry my whole life, but I could not share it with anyone. I didn't want to feel stupid when others pointed out all the mistakes. I always took their corrections personally, and I really thought that my grammar and spelling mistakes were a reflection of my intelligence. I went so far as to make sure that I avoided jobs that involved writing. Now, that was incredibly tricky, and talk about limiting choices!

I hoarded this idea and defended it to myself until December of 2009, when I finally thought, *So what? I can write purely because I want to.* It was in that moment of knowing that I let myself write this book. I did not worry about any of my old limiting beliefs; I did not edit myself as I went along; I just let the words flow. Every tear I had ever shed about my lack of writing skills now filled the cup I drank from. I could feel gratitude for my hoarding mindset; it had held me back until I was truly willing to create this dream. Once I became grateful for where I was in life, there was no stopping the writing. It opened the door to a new-found love and trust within myself, which enabled me to share my thoughts and connected me to everyone.

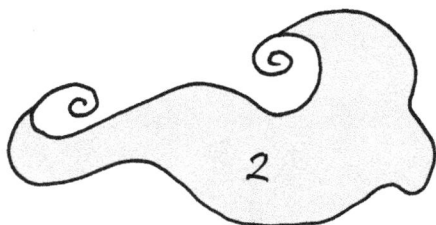

Dreaming

I'm driving in a car
But I'm sitting in the backseat.
In the dream I know I'm the one driving
In the dream I start to freak out

How can I be driving from the backseat?

Crust

The crust is the foundation of your pie and is created with ingredients that only you can choose. I trust you are recognizing more ingredients that you love and that fill your days with passion. Hopefully, you are now feeling confident about any changes you've made in your life. Maybe you are also trying out the idea of holding back on judging others, even if you don't like their ideas.

Your choices should be guiding you toward the kind of pie you currently desire. Don't worry about last year or next month; different times call for different pies. Accepting where you are at this moment opens you up to loving the possibilities that are right in front of you.

Tutor

You don't have to count on anyone else or even do anything. There is no right or wrong way. There are no hoops to jump through, except all the ones you would like to give yourself. All you have to do is decide which pie (idea) you desire, and then create it.

I can hear you already. You're thinking it has to be more complicated than that, and excuses for not trying are rising up in your mind. But, please, remember, we are only making pie. It is as simple as that.

Let's take a little trip to open your mind to a broader perspective on familiar situations. It's a nice day for a plane ride. We're in mid-flight when the air mask falls from the overhead compartment. You know the drill; you've heard it many times. Put on your own mask before trying to help someone else with theirs. You know what you're supposed to do, but your mind runs right over to the judgment field, where it's still really comfortable, and starts throwing all kinds of ideas at you (like throwing pie, it can get really messy):

- No, my kids really do come first.
- I wonder if we still get lunch?
- Why is this happening to me?
- This had better not make me late.
- I can't go anywhere without something going wrong.
- This should not be happening.

Your thoughts kick over into your voice, and now you are shouting out, getting others worked up, too. You get lost in all the noise and commotion, forgetting the real focus: breathing! Your thoughts have been interrupted like commercials during a TV show, answering the phone while making supper, or trying to drive from the backseat.

The same situation without all those interruptions goes something like this. You are mid-flight when you notice that the air feels heavy. An air mask falls from the compartment overhead; you reach for it, put it on, and take a deep breath. That feels better. You now decide to help those within your reach who need it.

In both scenarios, the desire is the same: to be able to breath. Sometimes, we get wrapped up in secondary things. We forget what our desire is. My desire in writing this book is to remind you that you already know what you love or desire. Just stop making judgments and hoarding old ideas. Better yet, put them in the garbage, for there is no room for them in a good pie crust. Love makes the strongest foundation, and that is not just true in pies.

Inherent

A bird focuses on three things: food, shelter, and a mate. A bird is always successful, unless it goes against its own nature—like refusing to look for food, or building a nest next to something that would consider it lunch, or picking a snake as a mate.

We humans have pretty much the same focus as the bird, except that we've arranged to pay for most things. We've done this to free up time to do what we love.

We pay someone else to grow our food; it saves time, and we don't have to worry whether the crop will be good. We can get more variety this way. We can even get food from another country.

When it comes to shelter, we pay someone else to build it. It saves us time, so we can do what we love. With so many helping hands, we don't have to worry about the size of the job. We can even add extra rooms.

And then there is the issue of picking a mate. In North America, the possibilities for finding a mate are endless, and, as with food and shelter, we can pay someone to do the looking for us. It saves us time to do what we love. We don't have to worry that we might pick the wrong person. We have a bigger variety to choose from. We can even pick someone from another country. So, we think we've freed up all this time to do the things we love; but, instead, we end up working harder than ever to pay for all of it, and we have completely forgotten what we love.

Thankfully, like birds our inherent nature is always with us, we select ideas and things around us to remind us of our passions. Your everyday life is really directing you. Whether you notice your natural tendencies or not, they are always close at hand. Next time you are dusting, take note of the objects you have acquired and how you feel about them.

Taste

Sometimes the simplest idea strikes you and sticks with you, even though you might not notice it or you seem to have forgotten about it. In my life, it's played out like this. I read the story of *The Little Prince*, where a little prince comes to Earth, looking to understand the nature of love. He travels to many planets looking for his answer, which he finally finds in the desert with the help of a downed pilot. During his quest, the little prince speaks of a rose that he's left on his own planet.

As I read this book, I focused personally on this rose. The thought that filled my mind was this: How could the rose find love, stuck in the ground where it was? For years, I carried this thought in my head. Although the idea would sometimes get lost, it would always come back to me. That idea set me in motion. I looked everywhere for the answer, but not until 2009 did I find it.

The answer was inside of me. For all those years, I had actually been in pursuit of a true understanding of love. It seemed that everything and everyone had been trying to help me. Love was the underlying message of every book I read, every person I met, and the direction I took in life.

For those of you stuck on the phrase "looking to understand the nature of love," here's what I mean by it. I did not really understand how love worked. I knew what it felt like, but within that great feeling, something was missing. That missing element was me. I came to this understanding the day I fell head-over-heels in love with myself. That moment changed everything. I was no longer looking outside myself for the answer; I *was* the answer. It did not matter were I was. My personal tastes, ideas, and ingredients were always nudging me along, constantly showing me my love. My internal love could be seen in every outward expression. I just didn't recognize it.

We always know the flavor of pie we would love to try next, but we forget that we can trust ourselves in the same way when it comes to making bigger decisions, too. Trust your own internal taste.

Defending

I must say, we are all in such a hurry to find what we want, that, if it takes any amount of time, we get side-tracked, and it seems as if we have lost our way. We just can't remember what we were doing or thinking when we veered off the path. You end up taking a summer job that lasts for seven years or a field trip that takes six months. You go for car rides, just for fun—and end up taking unexpected detours. You wonder, *Where did that husband and child come from?* Essentially, these moments are the best parts of your life—the living parts. They are excellent opportunities to practice making choices, adding and subtracting ingredients to adjust your personal preferences. If you are as lucky as me, you have also learned that you do not have to defend your individual taste.

I met a man from Egypt while waiting for the bus. He had moved to Canada when he got cancer. One of his children is a doctor here. He had come for help, and, on his journey, he was "born again," in his words. He had survived cancer twice and believed that Jesus had saved him both times. He wanted me to believe in Jesus, but it was more than that; he wanted me to believe in Jesus in exactly the same way he did. He said there were practices I should be following, places I should be going to, rituals I should be doing.

Finally, after going on for quite some time, he asked me, "What do you really believe in?" My heart raced, and I felt a sense of panic. I was trying to put my thoughts into words, when I came to the realization that he didn't really care about my choices. He had already judged them to be incorrect, and, in trying to prove his own ideas, he was ready to use whatever I said against me. I smiled to myself. *So, he only likes apple pie*, I thought, *but it's not just apple pie. He also has rules that dictate the best way to eat it.*

I smiled at him and said, "I understand your beliefs and how happy you must be to have found what you're looking for. How kind of you to try and share that with people you meet." He was a bit confused by this answer, but, with just a bit of a stumble, he got right back to his focus. He decided that the best way to help me was to pray for me, which I was happy to accept. The truth is, I like apple pie every now and again, and I don't mind it store-bought, homemade, hot, cold, with ice cream, or even with a piece of cheese.

I do not need to defend my choice of pie; all pies are yummy and lead to the same place. We can each accept another's idea of pie, but that does not mean we have to live it. Living the ideas you love and being open to others just means that, later today, you may discover you like chocolate drizzled over your apple pie.

If you are not defending your ideas against someone else's judgment, you are not trapped by one idea, and they are not trapped by yours. If you meet someone like this again, you can have a completely different conversation. There is nothing more enjoyable than expanding on something you already love, making it even greater.

Dreaming

I'm in a car going very fast
as I look down the hill we are on
I see obstacles moving directly
into our path
I realize the speed limit
is only fifty and we are doing ninety
I also now realize I'm in the front seat
but on the passenger side.
I say slow down, you are going too fast
closing my eyes.
I don't want to see the ill-fated impact
nothing happens
I open my eyes again
we are back on the top of the hill
I see obstacles moving directly
into our path
I realize the speed limit
is only fifty and we are doing ninety
I also now realize I'm in the front seat
but on the passenger side.
I say slow down, you are going too fast
closing my eyes.
I don't want to see the ill-fated impact
nothing happens
I open my eyes again
we are back on the top of the hill....

Filling

Are you starting to see where this thought might be taking you? Do you see where you might have made pie before and ended up with a filling you really did not like? Life likes to give us repeat performances, so we can test ourselves and see if last year's ideas are really what we want again. Keep your filling options open.

Substitute

One of the new pie fillings I tried was meditation. There are many forms of meditation—almost as many as there are pie flavors. But, like everything else, if meditation is something you might like to add to your ingredients, look around for one that will best fit your current needs. I chose a retreat that was ten days long, with ten hours a day of meditation. There were only a few simple rules: no food after noon, no books, no pens, no paper, and—what would become my favorite and most cherished rule—no talking. At first, the no pen and paper was the hardest. I was used to jotting down my ideas; every cloud is a poem, and there were many beckoning me.

Most people's fears seemed to be centered on not talking. Of all the worries I had about going on this retreat, the one that never crossed my mind was whether or not I would be able to "sit" for ten hours a day. I guessed if I could sit in front of the TV every night for hours on end, I would be able to do this. Mercifully, this fearful thought did not enter my mind until I got to the retreat and was about to sit for my first hour. Thankfully, meditation is another opportunity to open your mind on many levels; this includes recognizing the potential ways for sitting comfortably.

The possibilities were as diverse as the individuals. The first judgment I shed was the idea that there was a right and wrong way to sit. Some people sat without anything; some used cushions, balls, rolled blankets, blocks of foam, pillows, kneeling boards, and even chairs. Are you remembering that no judgment equals endless possibilities? It was like poetry to my eyes, and, yes, my body was also pretty happy to see the abundant ways of sitting. For the first few days, I was really just working out some judgments— some preconceived ideas I had about meditation—and doing my best to let them go. My little judge asked me every hour of every "sit": *Are you doing this right? Do you really think it's okay to be doing it like this, sitting like this? Are you thinking too much?* (Of course, we can all see the answer to that last question.)

But there came a day when, forty-five minutes into the hour, my mind realized that I was sitting, my body was doing exactly what it needed to be doing, and my mind had been silently observing my breath flowing in and out—nothing more, no questions asked. At this moment, joy washed over me, and my mind started to thank my body. I was so elated for my body, the pride was overwhelming; the body accepted the praise and sent just as much back to my mind. Waves of delight just kept crashing over me.

I was starting to have a hard time breathing. The intensity was getting stronger and stronger; tears were spilling from my eyes. I was only saved from this emotional train running through me by the gong signaling that the hour was up. After four days and forty-six hours of meditation, I had experienced success! I had just spent forty-five minutes in a complete state of quiet—quiet mind, quiet body. For forty-five minutes I had simply existed as a breathing, sitting, "being"—nothing more and nothing less. Even just writing this, my body and mind are running back to that amazing time. The nothingness of those moments were, and are, exceptional and incredibly empowering. The new "lightness of being" I felt, was like one of those pie fillings that are so fluffy, you think you could suck it up through a straw.

Substituting something new for something you have always done is like taking a deep breath in a pie shop. It awakens you to a sensation inside yourself. What flavor are you longing for?

Instinctive

Nature leaves room for everyone to just be. Nature can be a metaphor by which we observe life, but it seems we have forgotten how to look at it. Everything in nature is telling us a story, no matter what we look at—sea, sand, sky, birds, bugs, leaves, rocks, trees, flowers, or snow. What is the story?

Does the story say that there are no worries? That life is plentiful and abundant? That everything has its place? That life dies out and renews? What about the freedom to move about and transform?

Clouds do not ask if we would like shade, rain, or clear skies; they just shift and change as they will. No one doubts that clouds may run out or that there are too many one minute and not enough the next. We do not weep when they modify their shapes. We know it to be their nature. We do not cry if they are out of sight, or grieve that we will never see the same cloud twice. No matter what contour clouds take, we always recognize them. We never agonize about their feelings or judgments. We let them be. That is how nature reminds us daily about how life is. If we could view each other as clouds, then being ourselves would be as easy as pie.

Comprehension

I had spent the evening not feeling right about my scuba diving sessions. I was judging myself, and I was not coming up with any positive assessments. I had lost my confidence. I know exactly when I lost it, too. It was when I believed the disappointment in Robert's eyes.

We had been underwater, practicing buddy breathing, when I gave him back the alternate regulator before I had relocated my own. Now, there are two ways to search for your regulator. The first way is to tilt to the right and use your right arm to make a large circular motion; if the regulator is not caught up anywhere, the hose will cross over your arm. The other way is to reach up behind you, find the attached end, and follow the hose to the regulator. I had completely forgotten the second option. Twice, I tried to sweep my arm around to meet it, with no success. At this point, I really needed to take a breath so I just grabbled my spare air and breathed in … ah … and at that same moment, I felt Robert's judgment. It shot toward me and filled my senses. His eyes showed his disappointment. I let this feeling fill my body, and I became dissatisfied with myself, too. I stopped thinking of myself as a student learning something new and just wallowed in the thought that I couldn't do this.

The next morning, I woke up with this thought still in my head. I knew it was serving no purpose. I began searching to find a confident thought, but I was using my logical mind, and it was like solving a puzzle. I had all the pieces, but there was no picture to work with. I knew what self-confidence should feel like, but on this day, I could not get there from where I was. I toyed with the idea all morning. I was going diving that afternoon, and I did not want to take this feeling with me.

As we waited outside for our ride, it began to rain. We moved under the roof line for shelter. An old local man joined us to get out of the rain. I smiled at him. He was a few feet away and said something to me. I smiled again, though I couldn't really hear him. When he spoke again, I walked over to him. He asked where I was from, and, within a very few minutes of small talk, he said to me, "The important thing in life is to love yourself, then God, then your kids, and then anyone else you choose to love."

I could feel my mind shift; it was the answer I'd been looking for. "Love yourself" is always the answer, but sometimes, in the moment, you need to be reminded of it—like when your regulator hose escapes you. As soon as I started to think, *love yourself,* everything fell back into place. When you're in a state of love, you can't think or say judgmental or negative thoughts about yourself or anyone else. Instead, you see all the wonderful things you have done; you're grateful for your body and mind and for the amazing things they have helped you accomplish. My mind raced through all the thoughts of gratitude I had for myself, and then on to Robert, who wanted so much to teach me. I realized that all he wanted was for me to feel comfortable underwater—to feel that way even if I ran out of air. What an astounding idea to try to teach someone: that at sixty, eighty, or more feet underwater, you will be okay if something happens to your air source. That there are other possibilities for breathing underwater, you just have to relax and remember them.

There are always possibilities, if you are not judging the moment. No matter what the situation is, there is always more than one option. I hope you're also getting the idea that I'm filling my pie with love, because it's not just for the crust.

Liberation

Liberation is just suspending your judgment about any situation and admiring all the possibilities in it. In my life, both Daniel and I have a willingness to believe in Pocket Bear. This is a small wooden bear that fits into the palm of your hand. I gave Pocket Bear to Daniel in the early eighties when he was backpacking through Europe. I gave him the bear to watch over him and to keep him from being alone. He could just reach into his pocket, and there would be Pocket Bear, keeping him company. Daniel traveled for months with the bear in his pocket, and he was very pleased with him. Pocket Bear kept him safe on every adventure, and Daniel was never alone. We both started to realize that, if Pocket Bear was with us, the trip was smooth and easy. Without him, there was always something taking up our time that we would rather not deal with.

So, Pocket Bear became a travel necessity for a successful journey. Over the years, we told people about him, and, inevitably, they would want to travel with him. Pocket Bear worked for everyone, because our belief in him was so strong that others were willing to believe, too. A dear friend even made Pocket Bear his own homemade passport; which was very helpful in documenting all his destinations, as he is a very well-traveled bear.

My point here is that everyone was willing to be open to Pocket Bear. They trusted in him; they suspended their judgment and just went with the possibility that this little bear might take them on a trouble-free journey. And, after twenty years of travel, Pocket Bear just gets better and better.

You can believe in anything you want. What idea would you like to liberate? Is there an idea you keep running into that you promptly try to ignore? See if you can find one new possibility in it or a new way to view it. But, before you judge it, try it; the nature of a complete thought is that easy. Remember, all you have to do is get an idea. Work through it to create it, and then, upon completion, you decide the level of enjoyment you received. That conclusion will propel you on to your next idea. It is only when we work through an idea to its completion that the next idea has room to show up.

Now, I know some of us get an idea and judge it before experiencing it, but, without working through it, an idea can never be completed. It is like making a pie with no filling. The pie has the potential to be any flavor, but, without a making a choice, it will always remain just a crust.

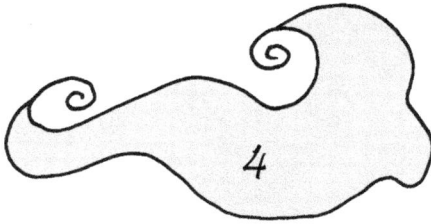

4

Clouds

The clouds were breathing in the moisture of the sea,
great deep breaths.
Slowly their color changed as they filled themselves fuller and
fuller
their bellies were swollen and gray
So full of drops: there was no room
for sunlight to play.
When the clouds were so full and could
not fit another breath, they exhaled, slowly at first, like
a misty kiss and then within seconds the air was filled in with
great big drops, warm and wet like a puppy's lick.

If you had chosen this time
to go and make a cup of tea,
you would have missed everything.
The sky from the living room window
would be blue again and the clouds
large, white and fluffy with the sun peeking through.
Only in glancing at the lawn chairs now puddled with water
would you know anything happened.

Baking

If you have come this far, you can stop worrying; you have already made your pie choice, it is in the oven, and it smells delicious. You can be proud of the effort you've put into your ingredient selection. You've looked internally and externally and made choices based on your own individual taste. While the pie is baking, maybe there's time for a little meditation or a dip in the sea. There is so much to enjoy in life.

Mentor

I was so enjoying my new appreciation for myself that I sat myself down and started to meditate. Almost immediately, I felt a small pain in my back. I knew it would go away, because, for the past week, that was exactly what had happened. You have a pain, and it comes and goes; you have an itch, and it comes and goes; you have a tingle, and it comes and goes. So, I let my mind rest briefly on the pain and then moved my attention elsewhere. But the spot called me back.

I thanked the painful spot and told it that I would come back to it. I tried to continue with my meditation, but now the spot was pulsing. I drew my full awareness to it. It was defiant and getting stronger. I decided I would move very slowly to the left, which just made it grow larger and throb more. In a discourse the night before, the teacher had spoken of finding the real root of our problems, not just skimming the surface, because a problem that's removed without pulling out the root comes right back. (This sounds like judging and defending, where we repeat the same conversations over and over.)

By this time, I was in a great deal of pain. I slowly moved forward, thinking it would help. It just created a sensation of having something literally pulled from my body. I decided it must be a root. If I could pull the pain out of me, it would remove the core of all my problems. So I sat back into the pain and used every fiber in my body to accept it. I tried to feel it without craving or aversion, to just be with it, to observe it—and, just as I came to this place of observation, the hour was up. I was so relieved, I got up and left the hall. The pain came with me, but it was no longer pulsing or as sharp.

After a short break, I returned to the hall for the evening discourse. For that hour, I was supposed to just sit comfortably. So, I sat back down, and instantly I felt shooting pain in the same spot on my back. I reached behind me to rub the spot and discovered something small and hard pressing into the back of my hand. I pulled my back cushion onto my lap, and there in the middle of it was my "mentor"—teaching me cause-and-effect. The cause was a string, knotted to one side of the cushion's middle. I had been sitting with this knot firmly pressed into my back.

Yes, there was a big smile on my face. I sat listening to the speaker while my fingers untied the knot. I pulled the string from the pillow, tied the two ends together, and slipped the loop onto my wrist. I gave it to myself as a present to remind me that, in nature, everything comes and goes, and, in our bodies, everything comes and goes; but we should not ignore something that is rubbing us the wrong way. We need to look for the root, look for the real cause, and, in doing so, we will be working toward that complete thought.

Intrinsic

When I get hot, I love to cool off in the ocean. I adore the feeling of water cooling me off, inch by inch. The heat melts away from me as I relax and lay out in the water. I love the feeling of floating. Sometimes Daniel holds my hand, and I call this kite-flying, because that is how I think a kite must feel—floating, but connected—so there is just this little tugging sensation. It is so comforting to know that you are free to float but are still held safe.

I love watching the clouds move from this vantage point. The light is constantly changing on them. They have a poetry to them that I am collecting. As I watch the clouds, I have come to realize that they are the only things in this world that we expect to change. We are so caught up in our lives that we think we never change, and one day seems just like the next. We forget that we are also in a constant state of movement. Our ideas change constantly; but, of course, if we don't take any action toward them, they will stay in the same place. Judging outcomes before creating them leaves us with nothing more than an idea (pie crust). This stops the creative flow of amazing possibilities that surround us. In nature, we can't move forward by standing still.

While you are waiting for your pie to bake, let your intuition guide you, and ask yourself what action is drawing your attention.

Knowledge

It is amazing to me how the body has learned to play tricks on the mind in its quest to be loved. There are creams, butters, gels, and oils that the body has convinced the mind to spread all over it. When the body wants a loving touch, when we are lost in some incomplete thought and are in the midst of forgetting our very nature, the body says, *Hey, my hands are dry; my legs are dry*. And, without really thinking about it, the mind complies, instructing the hands to slather the richest of creams onto the body, each caress a gentle nudge toward this minute in time. The body feels nurtured and loved, and this energy is sent to the mind, which then calms down and comes back to the present moment.

The body also reminds us that we understand life through action, and living is all about experiencing life, letting ourselves feel new emotions stirred up by our actions, seeing new potentials to explore. Did you know that the Library of Congress has eighteen million books? But that did not stop me from wanting to personally discover what it feels like to write a book, publish it, and see others enjoy it. It is through experiencing something for ourselves that we grow, bringing us love and joy in ways we can only appreciate through achievement. It's just like making a new flavor of pie. Yummm....

Release

I have come to understand something important. Once you feel the power of loving yourself—loving not just a small part of you but your complete mind, body, and soul—then love is like a giant eraser. It wipes out negative thoughts, the need for competition, the feeling that something is lacking, the feeling of not being good enough, the insecurities that stop you from trying something new. Self-love is a magic key; and, as with any key, when we first get it, we might forget it somewhere or lose it for a little while. But something always brings it back to us, and the times of forgetting it or losing it become fewer and less often. Every day is an opportunity to live in a state of self-love, from your inside, out.

I have always believed I could not trust women, because a female who was close to me lied a lot and was unable to be true to her word. I viewed all women through her example. When I released it and let in new possibilities, I realized that this person had grown up with many hardships and was really afraid to make a mistake. She could not be true to her word, because, each time she made a choice, she regretted it; and then she'd make another choice, which she would also come to regret.

To change my perception and let in new ideas, I had to step back and view her as a cloud. She was not really lying as I had judged it; she was merely being herself, drifting and changing her mind, moving from one idea to the next, letting her thoughts waft everywhere, following them but never completing them.

She was simply riding the currents. By liberating her from my label of untrustworthiness, I learned about the power of being true to myself, about the authority of words and the expectation they can hold. In setting this woman free as a cloud, I, too, am free. I'm grateful that words have become more significant to me because of this experience, which has also become a catalyst for helping me recognize the importance of completing my thoughts. Following thoughts to completion has released me to use words in a stronger and more important role than just in conversation.

Love flows when we find the gratitude in a situation; gratitude is easy to share; sharing opens the possibilities to new love—which brings us gratitude, which is easy to share, which brings us new possibilities to love....

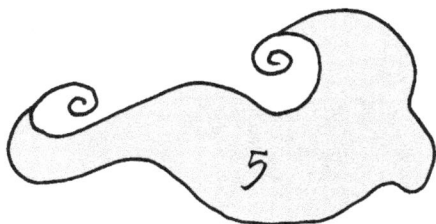

Clouds

Anytime of the day you could hear J-me say
"that is my favorite cloud"
all day, everyday
J-me never tired of looking at the
sky and every cloud was amazing
J-me never pointed, never looked
directly at any one cloud,
which was nice because
then when I looked up
I too would see a favorite cloud and answer
"me too"

Enjoying

Enjoying fresh-baked pie is something most of us will take time to sit and savor. There are so many warm, loving images that come to my mind when I think of pie. I really wanted to share this journey with you to help you remember to love yourself. It is one of the simplest things to say, but one of the hardest to achieve. Every action you allow yourself to do out of joy or love will bring you one step closer to loving your whole being. And that is all that really matters.

Master

It is so rare that we ever finish a thought (except in cooking), because, as we think about one idea, we open up more ideas; and then we start to talk about it, which opens up even more ideas, which are really endless. Then, when we get side-tracked and forget what the first thought was, how can we complete it? As long as we never complete a thought, we lose track of where we are in the world. We start to look to others for validation, instead of allowing others to be a gentle nudge that reminds us of the loving beings we are. We want them around us constantly, confirming that we are okay, likable, and worthy; we want their opinions to be our opinions. We stop accepting ourselves and, instead, want everyone else to accept us first. This is when our friend Judgment comes out to play.

We all know that everyone has an opinion, and it is impossible to believe 100 percent of everything someone else believes. Just look at your ingredients list. Do you really want the same list for everyone? This is not a test, and copying answers is not necessary. There are a million trillion thoughts in the world. But there is really only one thought you have to complete: to suspend your judgment, stop hoarding every thought that ever came into your head, and follow your true nature. Will you admit that you are lovable just the way you are? That is the most important part of being you. Loving yourself makes you a complete thought, and life becomes as easy as pie.

Intuitive

Do you love yourself? If not, why not? What ideas are you hoarding about yourself? What judgment do you keep repeating about yourself? What part of your own nature are you holding back?

Let's make this as easy as pie. The kitchen is a place where we allow ourselves to be intuitive. We add and subtract from recipes all the time; we even make up our own. Sometimes, we really love what we have made and are so proud that we want to share it. Other times, a single bite sends the whole thing into the garbage.

I learned to cook late in life, unless you think forty-five is the right time to start. I had held myself back from the kitchen for all that time. I judged myself as incapable and hoarded any thought that supported the idea that I might be worthless in the kitchen. Do you see how this works? I was hanging onto the idea that being worthless in cooking made me just plain worthless! I would walk into the kitchen and think, *What do I want to make?* For some reason, pies always came to mind, but, for the most part, I could not think of a single thing to make.

Standing in my kitchen, I learned a great trick. I would suspend my judgment and release any ideas that I could not make something. Then I would ask myself, "What would Tracey do?" Now, Tracey is fearless in her kitchen. She brings in new inventions weekly. I asked her how she came up with all those ideas, and she said it was simple. She knew the foods she loved to eat, and she would start from there by adding a few new ingredients or a new twist on the old ones. Suddenly, the cooking possibilities were endless. Cooking really opened my mind to completing a whole thought, and each dish was an example of that completion: I needed to eat, I decided what to make, I created it, and I tasted it. In the tasting, I completed the idea by asking myself, *Did that work? Did I like it? Would I do it again?*

I didn't really even care if the result was only so-so, because I already knew what I might do differently the next time. It was just one more meal among many. Every idea that prevents you from loving yourself is like a meal not savored, but don't let that stop you. Feel free to try again. Ask yourself what you need in your life, decide on it, try to create it, and then see if you like it. Don't fool yourself into forming a conclusion before you complete your idea. When you have completed the idea then ask if it worked, if you liked it, would you do it again? Like cooking, success is never a guarantee; but in the creative experience, we always see a new idea on the horizon.

Maybe this next pie (idea) will be the one to really open your heart.

Awareness

I have found that the best way to make an idea stronger, or to release an idea that no longer holds true for me, is to be aware that I'm thinking it. Here is an exercise you can try:

Sit quietly.
Keep your eyes closed.
Just breathe normally.

Sit comfortably in a room with no distractions; turn off the TV, stereo, and phone. You could be sitting in a chair at a desk or on the bed, but don't lie down—unless you want to start with a nap. You can also sit on the floor with cushions and lean back into something. Put cushions under any body part that feels too much pressure. Just be as comfortable as you can, while still being relaxed and mentally alert. Each time you sit, make a mental note of which way was the most comfortable so you're moving and adjusting as little as possible. Sitting comfortably without moving helps you focus on your breathing.

Breathe with all your attention around your nose. Do not think to yourself: I'm breathing in and out. Instead, just try to feel your breath in and around your nose. The feelings can be tingling, itching, burning, or cold. Sometimes you'll feel nothing. Don't look for something to feel; just feel what is happening without judgment. If you lose your focus because your mind is taking you somewhere, then I want you to write your thoughts down on paper. You might want to categorize your thoughts as positive, negative, creative, or actions. If you keep coming back to the same thought, put a mark beside it to keep track of how many times you think of it. There are no right or wrong thoughts, and only you will see what you write. Once you have written everything down, take a deep breath or two to refocus your attention on the feeling in your nose area again. Continue practicing this exercise over the next few days until you feel comfortable sitting and you notice that your mind is running mainly over the same thoughts.

When you're ready to take the next step, look over your list of positive and negative thoughts. Beside each negative note, write a positive thought to replace it. You might already have a positive on your list that will work. Here's an example: I hate my arms. The positive replacement might be that I like my ability to create with my hands. You might discover that you have a deep-rooted idea like my past idea that all females lie. For those kinds of thoughts, you will need to be patient and gentle, playing with them to see if you can view them from the clouds or on the branch of a tree.

Maybe you will discover that you have already implemented a positive action to compensate for that negative idea. Now, all that's needed is to release the idea or person that's attached to it. The fastest way to release a negative action is to recognize that it helped to create a new, positive attribute in you. Let gratitude free you, and admire your amazing accomplishment.

When you've found a positive thought for every negative:

Sit quietly.
Keep your eyes closed.
Just breathe normally with your attention on your nose area.

Now, when one of your negative thoughts comes up, I want you to thank it. It could sound like this in your head: *I hate my arms.*

Oh, thank you, Mind, for that thought, but I love that I can carry a stack of favorite books. Then, take a deep breath or two to refocus your attention on the feeling in your nose area.

It is nice to become aware of your thought process. It also helps to take accurate stock of what is in your head. You can practice replacing negative thoughts every time you notice them. Thank it, reword it, breathe, and let it go. All the negative thoughts are ideas or thoughts that have not been completed; they want your attention, and they want to be completed. Like passing clouds, your thoughts pass by, helping you find your loving, whole self. They are pointing out areas that are not complete yet.

When you are ready to take the next step, look at your list and notice all the things you have listed in the Creative and Actions categories. Naturally, you may already be working on some of these—like doing the dishes or laundry. But there may be creativity or actions that you've put off, ideas like creating a painting, writing a book, creating a group of like-minded people, learning to sing, dancing, or sailing a boat. For each of these, I want you to take some time thinking about the idea and deciding what actions would make it happen. You don't have to take that action, but, being as detailed as possible, just note what you think is needed to start the ball rolling.

Releasing all the hoarded, incomplete thoughts in your head takes time, but it also takes pen and paper to really see where your thoughts have been taking you. The negative thoughts are just helpers to guide you. As you work through them, they open you up to the action and creative ideas that having been waiting their turn to fill your mind with fun and joy. Hmm ... that feels a lot like love!

Willingness

Willingness is not just believing in an idea—like Pocket Bear making travel pain-free. Willingness is when you believe so strongly in something that you act on it. Like taking Pocket Bear traveling or writing a book, it is one thing to believe you want the bear in your pocket or that you want to be a writer; but it is your own willingness that allows you to actually do it.

You should now be aware that loving yourself is the most important thought you have to complete, the most important question to answer. Are you willing to start from where you are at this present moment? Are you willing to see things in nature that encourage you? Are you willing to notice internal nudges in the form of all those things you surround yourself with, those things that echo your love? Are you willing to go a little further, to cut up your pie and see how you have been sharing it? If you are already in a state of self-love, your life should be filled with people, things, and activities you love. For the rest of us, there are changes we would like to make to our pie, and we have been side-tracked by a lot of incomplete ideas.

Here's an example of where I started from:

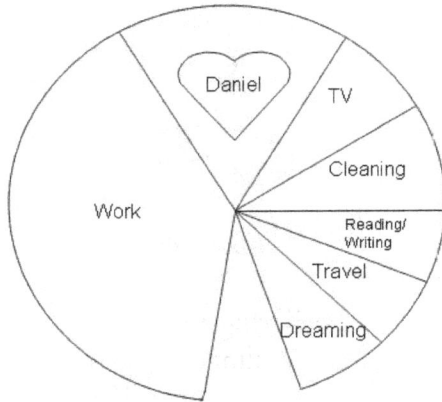

Pie chart with sections labeled: Daniel (in heart shape), TV, Cleaning, Reading/Writing, Travel, Dreaming, Work

You might wonder why I gave so much time to Daniel. The answer is simple, if I was busy doing things for him, I did not have time to look at my own life and how maybe I was not really living it.

As you can see, I have a missing piece. You might find that *you* are the piece missing from your pie. If you do not have an activity or time set aside that is just for you, then part of your pie is missing.

So, now you have acknowledged all of your positive attributes and changed your negative ones to constructive thoughts. You've made a list of the actions or creations you want to someday accomplish. (And you *should* try.) You have detailed some of the actions that would be required to get started. You have also recognized how you spend your time. Your life really is full and amazing, but would you like to go one piece further? Maybe it's time to choose and work through just one thing or activity that you may have been thinking about for a long time. Yes, I know. Sixteen ideas just popped into your head, but there is probably only one with which you are most willing to take the next step.

In my case, it was meditation. I actually had the specific retreat in mind. I was going back and forth, wondering, *Should I or shouldn't I?* Of all the ideas to cross my mind, this was the one I was most willing to make room for in my pie. And that's really all we are doing—making room in our lives so we can experience something new. We don't even have to worry about whether we will like it or not. It's just like trying a new pie flavor. So, I decided on meditation, and my next step was to register for the course. The class I picked would be in July, and I would be able to go online in April to sign up. Once I made that decision, I asked myself: Now that I know I'm going, what is the next step I'm willing to take?

For me, a very logical next move was to see a chiropractor. I'd had problems with my neck and shoulders for years. I had just lived with the pain, but I decided that, if I was meditating for ten hours a day, I did not want the pain to be my only thought. So, a few x-rays later, I scheduled a chiropractor to work through three problems. First, I had no neck mobility. (When you don't drive, you don't know that you can't shoulder-check.) Secondly, one hip was lower than the other. And, third, I was missing a little curve that should have been in my neck.

When you start to correct problem areas, unexpected benefits often show themselves. About a month into the treatments, I stopped having heartburn, and I started to sleep through the night. Daniel was also sleeping better, because I had stopped snoring. More sleep meant more energy, which was something I needed when I again asked myself what step I was willing to take next.

Immediately, I knew that I didn't want to come home from the retreat to a messy house full of junk. So, room by room, I performed a general purging of stuff. (Months after the retreat, I would be willing to do this on an even greater scale.) I soon discovered that paper was another thing I liked to collect; every room had tons of paper, and I'm not just talking about books and magazines, although there were plenty of those, too. Just working one room at a time was not as hard as I thought it would be; I actually started to enjoy it.

I was careful not to purge anything that did not belong to me, unless the owner was willing to part with it. To keep the process moving, I had a big, blue bin in each room for stuff that could be sorted later by the rightful owner. I want you to understand that, when you live in a family and you are making room in your pie to do something new, it is not your job to get everyone else to make room in their pies—unless it is their will to do so. Other people have their own pies, and how they choose to slice them up is totally up to them.

So, I worked through the few ideas I felt I needed to accomplish before the retreat—all in hopes that I would be pain-free and my mind would not be cluttered with all the other things I could have been doing for those ten days. The slices of my pie were starting to change. I had carved out some time from watching movies and TV to clean through my clutter. I had taken some Daniel-time and replaced it with time for myself in the form of going to the chiropractor. I would later fill this segment of my day with my new activity of meditation. As you may already have noticed, the meditation retreat was one of the best things I have allowed myself to do. I was able to complete my thought about the Little Prince's rose finding love, even stuck were she was. I hope you already know what I'm going to say: She found all the love she needed inside herself.

With my willingness to try something new, I had opened up new possibilities. I chose one possibility to try, suspended my judgment about it, stopped hoarding any ideas that were stopping me, and enjoyed finding a new slice of interest to add to my pie.

The process was so enjoyable that I opened up my willingness again when I got home. I had been leading the perfect life as a couch potato. I had to face the fact that, up until the meditation retreat, I hadn't actually admitted to myself that I had a body. I had let it sit dormant on the couch. My body had amazed me at the retreat, and I was now willing to put that to the test.

What was I willing to do next? Scuba diving came to mind! Daniel had been diving for years, and most of his time had been spent in, on, or under the water—or *trying* to be in, on, or under the water. Up to this point, I had been too afraid to try it myself. I picked scuba diving as the next slice of pie I would like to try, and I signed myself up for a class that gave me three months' lead time, hoping it would give me time to suspend my judgment and clear out all the ideas I was hoarding that were stopping me.

I eked out more time away from Daniel as I joined a gym. I had never worked out in my life, but I wanted to know that, when I made it to the ocean, I would be able to get in and out of the boat. I started with a weight-training program, and, when I grew confident that I still did have some muscles in my body, I started swimming, too.

I know some of you are saying that you don't have that kind of time, that your life is way too busy to add anything more, even if you wanted to. But that's just the point. When you are really ready to try something new—that one thing you have always wanted to do, but were afraid even to tell yourself—you will see creative ways to work it into your schedule. Maybe you have already noticed a section of time that you want to reduce—like watching TV or playing computer games. We mainly do these things to relax and unwind, but, if you are spending that same time learning French for your dream trip to Paris, you will find the time far more enjoyable, because it is to your exact personal taste.

Just as we know our favorite pies, we know our personal favorites in life; and, because they are preferences, they can never be wrong. So, look around you. What do you love? What ideas do you love to think about? What new slice of pie might you want to sample, just to see if it opens you up to loving yourself? You are working your way toward the love of your life—you—to live the life you love and love the life you live. Until you love yourself, your pie will never be whole. You can fill it with whatever you want, but without *you*, it's an incomplete thought.

I want you to know that everyone starts with a whole pie. We are each whole pies. Yes, there are times in our lives when we have given away pieces, and we think that we have gotten nothing in return. That's how our love of self goes missing. We think someone has to give it back to us. In a sense, that's true, but *you* are the person who has to give the missing piece back to you. You have been keeping yourself out of the picture. You haven't really given away anything; you have lost nothing; and every move you have made in life is perfect for you. Every struggle you've come through was made especially for you. There is one secret that you have been keeping from yourself, and it's this: You are amazing and worthy, and all the love you ever wanted for yourself is right there inside of you now. You just have to believe that you are more than worthy of it, and let yourself feel the love and joy that you are.

Remember, you don't have to act on any of this. Just know that when you are willing to take action, to complete something you love, that you really are opening yourself up to your own love. That is how it works, and it works this way for everyone.

Just like sharing your favorite pie with a friend, it's easy and fun.
And one piece leads to another.

Acknowledgments

Daniel W. for loving me and always giving me room to grow.
Lisa W. for showing me the power of an unconditional gift.
All my love and gratitude to my family and
friends, without you, I could never have reached
the amazing joy that is now my life.
Oprah Winfrey and Dr Wayne Dyer
as you encouraged others; I took it all to heart.
Alan Cohen and Bobbie Marchesso for sharing spiritual support
Abraham-Hicks Publications for opening my eyes
Louise Hay for creating Hay House radio and Balboa Press,
giving my dreams a place to flourish
Christine Moore for all her editing inspirations

Come play on the interactive web site
www.natureofacompletethought.com

love notes

---

love notes

_____

_____

_____

_____

_____

_____

_____

_____

_____

_____

_____

_____

_____

_____

love notes

_____

_____

_____

_____

_____

_____

_____

_____

_____

_____

_____

_____

_____

_____

_____

_____

_____

love notes

_____

_____

_____

_____

_____

_____

_____

_____

_____

_____

_____

_____

_____

_____

_____

_____

_____

love notes

_____

_____

_____

_____

_____

_____

_____

_____

_____

_____

_____

_____

_____

_____

_____

_____

love notes

_____

_____

_____

_____

_____

_____

_____

_____

_____

_____

_____

_____

_____

_____

_____

_____

love notes

_____

_____

_____

_____

_____

_____

_____

_____

_____

_____

_____

_____

_____

_____

_____

_____

_____